Character Education

Determination

by Lucia Raatma

Consultant:
Madonna Murphy, Ph.D.
Professor of Education
University of St. Francis, Joliet, Illinois
Author, *Character Education in America's
Blue Ribbon Schools*

Bridgestone Books
an imprint of Capstone Press
Mankato, Minnesota

Bridgestone Books are published by Capstone Press
151 Good Counsel Drive, P.O. Box 669, Mankato, Minnesota 56002
http://www.capstone-press.com

Library of Congress Cataloging-in-Publication Data
Raatma, Lucia.
    Determination / by Lucia Raatma.
    p. cm.—(Character education)
    Summary: Explains the virtue of determination and describes ways to show
it in the home, school, and community.
    Includes bibliographical references and index.
    ISBN 0-7368-1387-X (hardcover)
    1. Perseverance—Juvenile literature. 2. Determination (Personality trait)—Juvenile
literature. [1. Determination (Personality trait)] I. Title. II. Series.
BJ1533.P4 R32 2003
179′ .9—dc21
                                              2001007903

Editorial Credits
Megan Schoeneberger, editor; Karen Risch, product planning editor; Steve Christensen,
    series designer; Heidi Meyer, book designer; Alta Schaffer, photo researcher;
    Nancy White, photo stylist

Photo Credits
Capstone Press/Jim Foell, 6, 8, 10, 12, 20
Comstock, Inc., 4, 14
Corbis/Hulton-Deutsch Collection, 18
Corbis Stock Market/Peter Beck, 16
PhotoDisc, Inc., cover

1 2 3 4 5 6 07 06 05 04 03 02

Table of Contents

Determination

Determination is about setting and working toward goals. It means making a decision to do something and sticking to it. Learning how to swim takes practice. People with determination reach their goals.

decision
the result of making up your mind about something

Being Determined

Being determined means having willpower. A job you have started may seem very hard. It may take a long time. You keep trying when you are determined. You are determined when you work toward your goal no matter what.

willpower

strong determination; people with willpower do not allow their attention to move to something else.

Determination at Home

Perhaps your family is getting a new puppy. Be determined to care for your puppy. Read books about the type of dog you choose. Talk to other dog owners. Be sure to feed and care for your puppy. Show determination by doing these tasks without being asked.

Determination with Your Friends

You and your friends can set goals as a group. Maybe you have a puzzle to solve. Some of you can sort the pieces. Others can try fitting the pieces together. The puzzle may be difficult. Your group shows determination by working until the puzzle is finished.

Determination at School

Some of your school subjects may be difficult. You may think that you will never learn to subtract and add. Ask your teacher for help. You show determination when you work hard to learn new things.

Determination at Play

Learning to ride a bicycle takes determination. Other kids may seem to learn faster than you learn. You may fall and want to quit. You show determination when you try again.

Determination and Hobbies

Think of a hobby you want to try. Be
determined to learn about your hobby.
Maybe you want to start a stamp
collection. Learn about different types
of stamps. Find books at the library.
Set goals and work toward them.
Stick with your new hobby.

collection

a group of things or objects that
are gathered over a long period
of time

17

"It's kind of fun to do the impossible."
—Walt Disney

Determination and Walt Disney

Walt Disney liked to draw. He wanted to make cartoons. Many people thought his ideas were silly. But Walt was determined and did not quit. He worked hard to create many famous cartoon characters. Walt won many awards for his work.

create
to make something

Determination and You

Maybe you want to learn to play the piano. Or maybe you want a part in the school play. Determination means motivating yourself. Practice your skills. Decide to be good at whatever you choose to do. Being determined will help you accomplish your goals.

motivate

to encourage someone to do a task

Hands On: Reading New Books

Reading new books can be fun. Set a goal to read a new book each week. Use determination to accomplish your goal. Reading will become easier. You will learn about all kinds of things.

What You Need

An adult (parent, teacher, or librarian)
A library or bookstore
A dictionary

What You Do

1. Ask an adult to help you choose a new book. You can choose one about sports, an important time in history, or an interesting person.
2. Set aside 15 to 30 minutes each day to read. You could try reading after school or before you go to bed each evening.
3. Take your time with your book. Read as slowly or as quickly as you like.
4. Use the dictionary to look up words you do not understand.
5. Talk to an adult if you are having trouble. Other people sometimes can help you understand a book you are reading.
6. Think about the book when you are finished. Tell your friends whether you liked it or not. Then choose another one.

goal (GOHL)—something that you aim for or work toward; being determined helps you reach your goals.

hobby (HOB-ee)—something that you enjoy doing in your extra time

motivate (MOH-tuh-vate)—to encourage someone to do a task; you show determination when you find ways to motivate yourself.

practice (PRAK-tiss)—to do something over and over in hopes of getting better at it; determined people practice to learn new skills.

skill (SKIL)—the ability to do something well

willpower (WIL-pou-ur)—strong determination; people with willpower do not allow their attention to move to something else.

Read More

Lynch, Wendy. *Walt Disney.* Lives and Times. Des Plaines, Ill.: Heinemann Interactive Library, 1999.
Woodworth, Deborah. *Determination: The Story of Jackie Robinson.* Plymouth, Minn.: Child's World, 1999.

Internet Sites

Adventures from the Book of Virtues
http://pbskids.org/adventures
Amazing Kids!
http://www.amazing-kids.org
JustDisney.com—Walt Disney
http://www.justdisney.com/walt_disney

Index